HALLOWEEN

By Gail Gibbons

Holiday House · New York

TRICK OR TREAT

For Frances Lane

Library of Congress Cataloging in Publication Data

Gibbons, Gail.
Halloween.

Summary: Presents the many traditions associated with
the Halloween holiday, including making jack-o'-lanterns,
wearing costumes, trick-or-treating, and telling scary
stories.
1. Halloween—Juvenile literature. [1. Halloween]
I. Title
GT4965.G53   1984   394.2′693   84-519
ISBN 0-8234-0524-9
ISBN 0-8234-0577-X (pbk.)

OCTOBER 31

Halloween is celebrated on October 31st.

Many years ago there were people who believed that witches, ghosts . . .

goblins, and elves roamed the Earth on that night.

Some of these people made big bonfires to scare them away.

Later, October 31st was called All Hallows Even, which means holy evening. It was the night before a church festival called All Hallows or All Saints Day. All Hallows Even was shortened to Halloween.

Today many different things are done on Halloween. It is a time of fun.

Pumpkins are carved, and candles are placed inside them. When the candles are lit, the pumpkins glow. Sometimes they are called jack-o'-lanterns.

The word jack-o'-lantern comes from an old fable about a man named Jack, who was mean and stingy. When he died, he couldn't get into heaven. There wasn't anywhere he could go.

So he carved a turnip, placed a piece of hot, glowing coal in it, and roamed about at night. People called him Jack of the Lantern or Jack-o'-lantern.

Also, on Halloween costumes and masks are worn that look like witches, goblins, and ghosts.

Other kinds of costumes and masks are seen, too. People can pretend to be anything they want to be. It's make-believe.

Halloween decorations are put on doors and in windows.

Scarecrows appear on porches with harvest decorations.

Halloween used to be a time for playing tricks.

Nowadays, Halloween is a time for ringing doorbells and saying trick-or-treat.

Trick-or-treat bags are filled with Halloween goodies.

People have fun seeing the different costumes and having spooky visitors come to their homes.

Sometimes Halloween parties are given. There are decorations.

It is fun to guess who is who.

Scary stories are told.

Tasty party snacks are enjoyed.

Halloween games are played, too.

Bobbing for apples is an old English game.

At times there are Halloween plays . . .

and there might also be make-believe haunted houses for guests to go through.

In some places there are Halloween costume parades and contests.

Sometimes awards are given.

Halloween is for all kinds of make-believe and laughter, and for saying BOO!